I0418535

DELIVERANCE

STARTS WITH ME

An Interactive Journal and Devotional

CYNTHIA D. JOHNSON

DELIVERANCE STARTS WITH ME
An Interactive Journal and Devotional
Cynthia D. Johnson

All rights reserved. This book or any portion thereof may not be reproduced or used in any manner whatsoever without the express written permission of the publisher except for the use of brief quotations in a book review.
Unless otherwise noted, all scriptures were taken from the King James Version.

Copyright 2025 CI-54717460616
ISBN: 979-8-9985264-7-3
Printed in the U.S.A.

Table of Contents

DEDICATION

This book is lovingly dedicated to
every soul who has cried out to God
for help in the midnight hour and
waited in hope at dawn.

To those trusting God for deliverance,
may you find strength in every verse,
courage in every prayer, and joy in
knowing your Deliverer is faithful.

You are not alone. You are heard.
You are held.

— *Cynthia D. Johnson*

INTRODUCTION

Let me tell you a story of how life begins. Your story may be a bit different from mine, but all the principles are the same.

Every child born in this world was born in sin, shaped in iniquity. And from birth, the processes are basically the same... We cry, breathe, eat, poop and sleep.

Every mother or those who are caring for the baby learns to discern the cries of each child. When they're hungry, or sleepy.

By the time that child reaches a little under one year, it's either walking, or trying to walk, depending on their level skill sets or learning abilities.

The process continues. They walk, run, hop, skip, and jump. But each child is impressed with a set of impartations coming from their parents, siblings, neighbors, and communities.

By the time the child reaches Pre-K, or kindergarten, their personalities have already developed.

Habits are formed and mindsets are sharpened by those who have the greatest influence over their lives.

When habits are formed outside of Biblical principles, strongholds and soul ties emerge.

Some habits come forth in toddler years, some may come forth in preteen or puberty, but all are forming habits that will need for that child to be delivered at some phase of their life.

From childhood trauma to bullying, to teenage and adult experiences, deliverance needs to take place.

What is deliverance? In the Old Testament, deliverance is prominently featured in the story of the Israelites' liberation from slavery in Egypt. This historical event is not only a narrative of physical rescue but also a demonstration of God's power, faithfulness, and commitment to His covenant people.

The liberation from oppression and the subsequent guidance through the wilderness illustrate how deliverance was both a rescue from immediate physical danger and the beginning of a journey towards forming a holy community.

Deliverance is Divine Intervention:

The act of deliverance is portrayed as a direct intervention by God — an act that validates His sovereignty and care for those who are under His authority. This theme recurs throughout the Hebrew Bible, where God repeatedly saves His people from various forms of oppression, be it from invading empires, natural disasters, or internal strife.

Deliverance is Redemption from Sin:

In a broader theological context, deliverance is intimately connected with the concept of salvation. In the biblical narrative, especially in the New Testament, deliverance transcends physical rescue and enters the realm of spiritual redemption. It refers to being saved from the bondage of sin and the power of evil. For instance, Jesus' ministry includes acts of healing and exorcism, which are seen as symbolic acts of liberating individuals from demonic oppression and the spiritual death that accompanies sin.

Deliverance is Freedom in Christ: Many New Testament passages describe believers being "set free" or "delivered" as part of their new life in Christ. This freedom is often understood not only as liberation from past sins but also as an empowerment to live a life that reflects the values and teachings of Jesus. Deliverance, therefore, becomes a continuous process of sanctification—a daily reliance on God's grace to overcome spiritual challenges.

Deliverance as a Call to Trust and Obedience to have Faith and Dependence on God:

Biblical deliverance also emphasizes the importance of trust and obedience to God. The narratives show that deliverance comes through a relationship with God where faith plays a critical role. In the Psalms and prophetic books, prayers for deliverance are expressions of trust in God's ability to overcome even the most severe adversities. This aspect underscores that deliverance is not an automatic right but a response to a faithful relationship between the believer and God.

In The Lord's Prayer Jesus showed them a pattern of how they must pray:

The plea "deliver us from evil" in the Lord's Prayer (Matthew 6:13) encapsulates the idea that deliverance is an ongoing need for the faithful. This plea recognizes the ever-present nature of spiritual and moral challenges in human life and the necessity of divine assistance to navigate them.

Though Deliverance has a Dual Nature, it's both spiritual and physical:

The dual aspects of deliverance — both physical and spiritual — highlight a core biblical message: God is concerned with the whole person. This means that while He is mighty to save from physical dangers, His ultimate goal is to provide spiritual renewal and eternal life.

Community and Covenant:

Deliverance reinforces the idea of covenant relationships. The recurring deliverance stories remind believers that God's promises are not only about saving individuals but about forming a community that reflects His will and purpose on earth.

SUMMARY

Biblically, deliverance is a profound concept that:

Physically rescues individuals or communities from oppression and danger (as seen in the Exodus narrative).

Spiritually liberates from the bondage of sin and demonic influence, ultimately pointing to salvation through Christ.

Requires and strengthens faith, inviting believers into a dynamic relationship with God characterized by trust, obedience, and continual reliance on His saving power.

This layered understanding of deliverance continues to influence Christian theology and practice, underscoring both the immediacy of God's intervention in human affairs and the transformative, enduring nature of His redemptive work.

FIFTEEN DAYS OF DEVOTIONS

Morning & Night

Theme: God's Deliverance

DAY 1

Morning Devotion
Scripture:

"The righteous cry out, and the Lord hears them; He delivers them from all their troubles." — **Psalms 34:17 (NIV)**

Reflection:

God hears every cry from His people. He doesn't just listen — He moves to deliver. Whatever burden you carry this morning, you are not alone.

Prayer:

Lord, as I step into this day, remind me that You hear my every prayer. Deliver me from fear and anxiety and lead me into peace. Amen.

Day 1 Morning Reflection Question:

What burden am I carrying today that I need to cry out to God about?

_____

_____

_____

_____

_____

_____

_____

_____

_____

_____

_____

_____

_____

Night Devotion

Scripture:

"The righteous person may have many troubles, but the Lord delivers him from them all." — **Psalms 34:19 (NIV)**

Reflection:

Troubles are a part of life, but so is God's faithfulness. He doesn't promise a life without trouble — He promises deliverance through them all.

Prayer:

Father, thank You for Your protection today. I trust You with my troubles and lay them at Your feet tonight. Strengthen me for tomorrow. Amen.

Day 1 Night Reflection Question:

How did I see God's deliverance or protection show up today?

_____

_____

_____

_____

_____

_____

_____

_____

_____

_____

_____

_____

_____

DAY 2

Scripture:

"The Lord will fight for you; you need only to be still." — **Exodus 14:14 (NIV)**

Reflection:

Your greatest battles are won not by your effort but by your surrender. Stand still today and watch God work on your behalf.

Prayer:

Jesus, teach me the strength of stillness. Help me release my striving and trust that You are fighting for me. Amen.

Day 2 Morning Reflection Question:

Where do I need to stop striving and trust God to fight for me?

_____

_____

_____

_____

_____

_____

_____

_____

_____

_____

_____

_____

_____

Night Devotion

Scripture:

"For the Lord your God is the one who goes with you to fight for you against your enemies to give you victory." —

Deuteronomy 20:4 (NIV)

Reflection:

God never sends you into battle alone. Tonight, rest knowing He fought for you today and gave you the victory you couldn't achieve alone.

Prayer:

Lord, thank You for being by my side in every unseen battle. Let Your victory fill my heart with peace as I sleep. Amen.

Day 2 Night Reflection Question:

What battle did God help me face today that I couldn't have handled alone?

_____

_____

_____

_____

_____

_____

_____

_____

_____

_____

_____

_____

DAY 3

Morning Devotion

Scripture:

"He said: 'The Lord is my rock, my fortress and my deliverer.'" **2 Samuel 22:2 (NIV)**

Reflection:

Start today with the confidence that you are grounded in the Rock of Ages. No matter what shakes around you, your Deliverer remains firm.

Prayer:

My Rock and Deliverer, guide me today. Be my strong fortress when I feel weak and lead me safely through every challenge. Amen.

**Day 3 Morning Reflection Question:
In what area of my life do I need to
lean on God as my Rock and
Deliverer?**

_____

_____

_____

_____

_____

_____

_____

_____

_____

_____

_____

_____

_____

_____

Night Devotion

Scripture:

"He brought me out into a spacious place;
He rescued me because He delighted in me."

— 2 Samuel 22:20 (NIV)

Reflection:

God rescues you not out of obligation,
but because He delights in you. End
your day resting in His love and delight.

Prayer:

Father, thank You for rescuing me with
love. As I sleep, help me to remember
that I am deeply cherished by You.

Amen.

Day 3 Night Reflection Question: How did God show His delight in me today?

_____

_____

_____

_____

_____

_____

_____

_____

_____

_____

_____

_____

_____

_____

DAY 4

Morning Devotion

Scripture:

"For He has rescued us from the dominion of darkness and brought us into the kingdom of the Son He loves." — **Colossians 1:13 (NIV)**

Reflection:

You have been rescued from darkness. This morning, live boldly and joyfully, knowing you are part of God's glorious Kingdom.

Prayer:

Lord, thank You for rescuing me from the darkness. Help me walk today in the light of Your love and truth. Amen.

Day 4 Morning Reflection Question:

How can I live differently today knowing
I've been rescued from darkness?

_____

_____

_____

_____

_____

_____

_____

_____

_____

_____

_____

_____

_____

_____

_____

_____

_____

Night Devotion

Scripture:

"So if the Son sets you free, you will be free indeed." — **John 8:36 (NIV)**

Reflection:

Your freedom isn't temporary, it's eternal. Let the certainty of Christ's deliverance settle your heart as you end your day.

Prayer:

Jesus, thank You for setting me free. Cover me in Your peace tonight and renew my heart with hope for tomorrow. Amen.

Day 4 Night Reflection Question:

What specific freedom did I experience

today because of Jesus?

_____

_____

_____

_____

_____

_____

_____

_____

_____

_____

_____

_____

_____

_____

_____

_____

_____

DAY 5

Morning Devotion

Scripture:

"When you pass through the waters, I will be with you; and when you pass through the rivers, they will not sweep over you." —

Isaiah 43:2 (NIV)

Reflection:

The water may rise, but they won't drown you. Walk confidently today knowing God is with you in every situation.

Prayer:

Lord, thank You for Your presence through deep waters. Help me trust You completely today. Amen.

Day 5 Morning Reflection Question:

What deep waters or challenges am I facing
that I need God's presence in?

_____

_____

_____

_____

_____

_____

_____

_____

_____

_____

_____

_____

_____

_____

_____

_____

_____

Night Devotion

Scripture:

"No, in all these things we are more than conquerors through Him who loved us." —

Romans 8:37 (NIV)

Reflection:

Because of Christ's love, you are not just surviving—you are conquering. End the day with the joy of your victory in Him.

Prayer:

Father, thank You for making me more than a conqueror. May Your love strengthen me through the night. Amen.

Day 5 Night Reflection Question:

What victory can I thank God for before I go to sleep?

_____

_____

_____

_____

_____

_____

_____

_____

_____

_____

_____

_____

_____

_____

DAY 6

Morning Scripture:

"God is our refuge and strength, an ever-present help in trouble." — Psalms 46:1 (NIV)

Reflection:

You are my hiding place and my strength. I don't face today alone — You are my ever-present help.

Prayer:

Lord, be my strength this morning. Remind me that I am never without help when You are with me. Amen.

Day 6 Morning Reflection Question:

Where do I need to run to God as my refuge
instead of relying on myself?

_____

_____

_____

_____

_____

_____

_____

_____

_____

_____

_____

_____

_____

_____

_____

Night Scripture:

"In peace I will lie down and sleep, for you alone, Lord, make me dwell in safety." — Psalms 4:8 (NIV)

Reflection:

Tonight I rest because I know I am secure in You. I don't have to be afraid—Your peace guards my rest.

Prayer:

Father, thank You for safe shelter in Your presence. Watch over me tonight. Amen.

Day 6 Night Reflection Question:

Did I feel peace tonight? If not, what do I
need to surrender?

_____

_____

_____

_____

_____

_____

_____

_____

_____

_____

_____

_____

_____

_____

_____

_____

_____

DAY 7

Morning Scripture:

"The Lord is my shepherd, I lack nothing." — Psalms 23:1 (NIV)

Reflection:

With You leading me, I have everything I need. You supply my strength and guide my steps.

Prayer:

Jesus, thank You for being my Shepherd. Lead me to what I need today. Amen.

Day 7 Morning Reflection Question:

What do I need to trust God to provide for me today?

_____

_____

_____

_____

_____

_____

_____

_____

_____

_____

_____

_____

_____

_____

Night Scripture:

"Surely your goodness and love will
follow me all the days of my life..."
Psalms 23:6a (NIV)

Reflection:

Your goodness didn't leave me today.
You pursued me with love, and I saw it
in every small blessing.

Prayer:

Thank You, Lord, for following me with
goodness. Let me rest in Your love.
Amen.

Day 7 Night Reflection Question:

Where did I see God's goodness and love
follow me today?

_____

_____

_____

_____

_____

_____

_____

_____

_____

_____

_____

_____

_____

_____

_____

_____

_____

_____

DAY 8

Morning Scripture:

"The Lord is my light and my salvation—whom shall I fear?" — Psalms 27:1 (NIV)

Reflection:

You are my light today. I don't have to fear what lies ahead when You go before me.

Prayer:

Lord, shine Your light on my path today. Banish every fear from my heart. Amen.

Day 8 Morning Reflection Question:

What fear can I face head-on because the
Lord is my light and salvation?

_____

_____

_____

_____

_____

_____

_____

_____

_____

_____

_____

_____

_____

_____

Night Scripture:

"Though my father and mother forsake me, the Lord will receive me." — Psalms 27:10 (NIV)

Reflection:

Even if others turn away, You still receive me. You never abandon me.

Prayer:

Thank You, God, for accepting me completely. As I sleep, hold me close. Amen.

Day 8 Night Reflection Question:

How did God show me I was not alone today?

_____

_____

_____

_____

_____

_____

_____

_____

_____

_____

_____

_____

_____

_____

_____

DAY 9

Morning Scripture:

"Cast all your anxiety on Him because He cares for you." 1 Peter 5:7 (NIV)

Reflection:

You care about every detail of my life. I give You every anxious thought today.

Prayer:

Lord, I release my worry to You this morning. Carry what I cannot. Amen.

Day 9 Morning Reflection Question:

What anxiety do I need to cast on God right now?

_____

_____

_____

_____

_____

_____

_____

_____

_____

_____

_____

_____

_____

_____

_____

_____

Night Scripture:

"The Lord gives strength to His people;
the Lord blesses His people with peace."
— Psalms 29:11 (NIV)

Reflection:

Your strength sustained me today, and
now Your peace wraps around me like a
blanket.

Prayer:

Thank You for the strength to get
through today, Lord. Now bless me
with deep peace tonight. Amen.

Day 9 Night Reflection Question:

How did God strengthen or give me peace today?

_____

_____

_____

_____

_____

_____

_____

_____

_____

_____

_____

_____

_____

_____

_____

_____

_____

DAY 10

Morning Scripture:

"I sought the Lord, and he answered me;
he delivered me from all my fears." —
Psalms 34:4 (NIV)

Reflection:

When I seek You, You answer. You
quiet my fears and fill me with courage.

Prayer:

God, as I begin today, deliver me from
the fear that tries to paralyze me. I trust
You. Amen.

Day 10 Morning Reflection Question:

What fear has been silenced in my heart
because I sought the Lord?

_____

_____

_____

_____

_____

_____

_____

_____

_____

_____

_____

_____

_____

_____

Night Scripture:

"The Lord is close to the brokenhearted and saves those who are crushed in spirit." — Psalms 34:18 (NIV)

Reflection:

Even in my lowest moments, You are near. You don't run from my pain — you run toward it.

Prayer:

Father, meet me in places that still ache. Heal me as I rest tonight. Amen.

Day 10 Night Reflection Question:

When did I feel God draw near to me in a
low moment today?

_____

_____

_____

_____

_____

_____

_____

_____

_____

_____

_____

_____

_____

_____

_____

_____

_____

DAY 11

Morning Scripture:

"Do not fear, for I am with you... I will strengthen you and help you." — Isaiah 41:10 (NIV)

Reflection:

No matter what I face today, You are with me. I will not be shaken, for You are my strength.

Prayer:

Lord, strengthen me today and help me stand firm. I will not fear, because You are near. Amen.

Day 11 Morning Reflection Question:

What challenge am I facing that I need
God's strength and courage for?

_____

_____

_____

_____

_____

_____

_____

_____

_____

_____

_____

_____

_____

_____

_____

_____

_____

_____

Night Scripture:

"You will keep in perfect peace those whose minds are steadfast, because they trust in you." — Isaiah 26:3 (NIV)

Reflection:

As I fix my thoughts on You, peace fills me. Trust anchors my heart tonight.

Prayer:

God, thank You for perfect peace. Help me sleep with my mind stayed on You. Amen.

Day 11 Night Reflection Question:

Where did I feel God's peace guard my mind
tonight?

_____

_____

_____

_____

_____

_____

_____

_____

_____

_____

_____

_____

_____

_____

_____

_____

_____

DAY 12

Morning Scripture:

"Call on me in the day of trouble; I will deliver you, and you will honor me." — Psalms 50:15 (NIV)

Reflection:

You've given me an open invitation to call on You. Today, I choose to rely on Your help, not my own.

Prayer:

Lord, I call on You today. Deliver me from anything that distracts me from Your purpose. Amen.

Day 12 Morning Reflection Question:

What trouble am I facing today that I need
to bring to God immediately?

_____

_____

_____

_____

_____

_____

_____

_____

_____

_____

_____

_____

_____

_____

_____

_____

_____

_____

Night Scripture:

"My flesh and my heart may fail, but God is the strength of my heart and my portion forever." — Psalms 73:26 (NIV)

Reflection:

Even when I feel weak, You are the strength that never fades. You are enough for me.

Prayer:

Father, You are my portion. Let Your strength carry me through the night. Amen.

Day 12 Night Reflection Question:

In what way was God my strength when I

felt weak today?

_____

_____

_____

_____

_____

_____

_____

_____

_____

_____

_____

_____

_____

_____

_____

_____

DAY 13

Morning Scripture:

"He gives power to the weak and strength to the powerless." — Isaiah 40:29 (NLT)

Reflection:

I don't have to start this day strong—I just need to start with You. You empower me when I feel empty.

Prayer:

Lord, fill my weakness with Your power today. I receive Your strength right now. Amen.

Day 13 Morning Reflection Question:

Where do I feel powerless—and how can I let God's power fill that space?

_____

_____

_____

_____

_____

_____

_____

_____

_____

_____

_____

_____

_____

_____

_____

_____

Night Scripture:

"Even youths grow tired and weary, and young men stumble and fall; but those who hope in the Lord will renew their strength." — Isaiah 40:30–31a (NIV)

Reflection:

My hope is in You, and tonight I receive new strength. Tomorrow is already filled with Your grace.

Prayer:

God, thank You for renewing me. Restore me as I sleep tonight. Amen.

Day 13 Night Reflection Question:

How has hope in God renewed me today?

_____

_____

_____

_____

_____

_____

_____

_____

_____

_____

_____

_____

_____

_____

_____

_____

_____

DAY 14

Morning Scripture:

"Be strong and courageous. Do not be afraid... for the Lord your God goes with you." — Deuteronomy 31:6 (NIV)

Reflection:

I am not alone today. Your presence gives me courage and strength to move forward.

Prayer:

Father, I choose courage because You are with me. Help me face this day without fear. Amen.

Day 14 Morning Reflection Question:

Where do I need to be bold and courageous because God is with me?

_____

_____

_____

_____

_____

_____

_____

_____

_____

_____

_____

_____

_____

_____

_____

_____

_____

Night Scripture:

"He will cover you with his feathers, and under his wings you will find refuge..." — Psalms 91:4 (NIV)

Reflection:

I'm covered tonight—safe under Your wings. Your refuge is my place of peace.

Prayer:

Lord, thank You for covering me. Let me rest deeply in the shelter of Your presence. Amen.

Day 14 Night Reflection Question:

What does it feel like to be under the covering of God's wings tonight?

_____

_____

_____

_____

_____

_____

_____

_____

_____

_____

_____

_____

_____

_____

_____

_____

DAY 15

Morning Scripture:

"Let the redeemed of the Lord tell their story—those he redeemed from the hand of the foe." — Psalms 107:2 (NIV)

Reflection:

I have a testimony of deliverance. Today, I will live boldly as one whom the Lord has redeemed.

Prayer:

God, thank You for my story of rescue. Help me live and speak like someone who has been set free. Amen.

Day 15 Morning Reflection Question:

What part of my story today reflects God's redemption?

_____

_____

_____

_____

_____

_____

_____

_____

_____

_____

_____

_____

_____

_____

_____

Night Scripture:

"Then they cried to the Lord in their trouble, and he saved them from their distress." — Psalms 107:13 (NIV)

Reflection:

Every time I called, You saved me. You heard me in distress and pulled me out.

Prayer:

Jesus, thank You for answering me. As I sleep, let my heart rest in the peace of Your salvation. Amen.

Day 15 Night Reflection Question:

What distress or trouble did I cry out about—and how did God respond?

_____

_____

_____

_____

_____

_____

_____

_____

_____

_____

_____

_____

_____

_____

_____

_____

_____

BIBLICAL CONCLUSION

Throughout this devotional journey, the reader has encountered the truth that God is not distant—He is the Deliverer, the Refuge, the Strength, and the ever-present Help. His love reaches into every dark and difficult place and lifts the believer into His marvelous light. The same God who delivered Israel from Egypt, rescued David from the giant, and raised Jesus from the dead—is the same God who walks closely with every believer today.

Deliverance is not just about being rescued from danger; it's about being brought into purpose. It is not only freedom from sin, fear, or shame — but freedom to live in peace, joy, purpose, and the hope of eternity with Christ.

The ultimate act of deliverance was fulfilled through Jesus Christ. He gave His life to save sinners and rose again to offer new life to all who believe. If the reader has not yet made the decision to follow Him, today is the perfect time.

THE SINNER'S PRAYER

Dear Heavenly Father,
I come before You acknowledging
my need for salvation.
I believe Jesus Christ is the Son of
God,
That He died on the cross for my
sins, and rose again to give me
eternal life.
I confess my sins and ask for Your
forgiveness.
Jesus, come into my heart. Be my
Lord and Savior.
Deliver me from sin, shame, and
anything that has kept me bound.
I surrender my life to You.

Fill me with Your Holy Spirit and lead me in righteousness.

Today, I receive the gift of salvation.

I am saved, set free, and made new.

In Jesus' name, Amen.

ABOUT THE AUTHOR

Dr. C.D. Johnson

Dr. Cynthia D. Johnson is the creative force behind DSC Publishers, Inc., which has been owned and operated since 2008, began in Central Florida, and is now licensed in Georgia. She has built a team of outsourced vendors over the past 15 years.

She branched out in 2011 to go back to school. After thirty years of graduating High School, she pursued her undergraduate degree in "Early Childhood Development" and a master's in "Human Service Counseling," focusing on Public Policy & Blended Families. She recently received a Doctoral of Philosophy Degree in Christian ethics & Business Management.

Her company publishes every genre, from children's books to inspirational journals. Her clients mainly consisted of teachers, doctors, and pastors. Erotica books are the exceptions DSC will not publish.

Her educational background affords her, as an author and trainer, the ability to teach book publishing in groups or individual private workshops about the business. Dr. Johnson is a mother of two business-minded daughters, a son-in-law and five grandsons.

CONTACT

If you'd like to reach out with any questions, comments, or to purchase bulk orders and speaking engagements, feel free to contact me at:

support@dscpublishers.com

Social Media

FB @ DSCBookPublishing

www.ingramcontent.com/pod-product-compliance
Lightning Source LLC
Chambersburg PA
CBHW021130130626
46554CB00002B/943